FORCE

FORCE

Finding purpose and meaning in the pursuit of strength, discipline and responsibility

Juan Domínguez del Corral

Force
Finding purpose and meaning through the pursuit of strength, discipline, and responsibility

Self-help/Self-improvement

Cover design: Rebecacovers-
https://www.fiverr.com/rebecacovers

ISBN: 978-958-48-7646-1
Printed in Colombia by Imágenes y Texto Ltda.

For more information or to contact the author, please go to www.instagram.com/juandominguezdelcorral

FORCE

Noun

Definition of *force*

Strength or energy exerted or brought to bear: active power

"Everything can be taken from a man but one thing: the last of human freedoms - to choose one's attitude in any given set of circumstances, to choose one's own way."

-Viktor E. Frankl

FORCE

Contents

Before you read

Let's straighten things up before you begin reading. This is not an attempt to brainwash you into thinking what I think or believing what I believe. It doesn't benefit me if you believe me or follow my advice. However, I think it may benefit YOU, which is exactly the reason I set out to write this book in the first place. I encourage you to disagree with me on some aspects. I encourage you to challenge my viewpoints. It is from disagreement that great ideas can be created, and that we can become better. I also hope that you agree on some things, and that they help you turn into a better version of you, and to achieve the life that you want.

Don't ever think that it is okay to point fingers at others and blame them for your circumstances. You are responsible for your life, and you are not a victim of your fate. Even those that have been unjustly treated, that have endured the greatest pains, can choose to rise from those experiences and accomplish great things. Suffering is a part of life, in fact, it's essential to the experience of living. Treat it as such, and you will rise above levels that were previously unreachable to you. True greatness and true happiness is reserved for those that experience the greatest suffering, and fight through it. Fight for your happiness, fight for your life and never let yourself be convinced that there are levels above which you cannot rise due to your race, gender or any other banal characteristic.

This is not a practical guide; this is also not a philosophical work or merely a critique of today's society. This book is meant to be a wakeup call for you, so that you can, while reading, realize that the way to get what you want out of life lies not in demanding it from someone else, but on going out there and taking it, that the way to a happy life is not found by turning on the auto-pilot and then following the herd while constantly pointing fingers and complaining about everything, and that, rather, it is found in accepting responsibility for your circumstances, setting goals and defining dreams, becoming strong and standing tall and proud, not letting anything keep you from achieving and directing every action and thought towards the completion of your dreams.

Introduction

We've been lied to. They've been feeding us feel-good nonsense and I'm personally sick of it. All we see are lies, and weakness, and complaints, and irresponsibility, and we're being told it's normal. As if our life was someone else's responsibility, as if our failures were someone else's fault. As if we should feel guilty when someone feels offended or attacked by our actions and our perception of how things are, and how they ought to be. Rich people are called arrogant, and successful people obviously cheated and screwed people over in order to achieve whatever material success they have, is what we're told. Anyone that has more of anything than someone else should share it with them, because "we're all human" and "we should all be equal", and because "why does someone need ten million dollars?" All we see are excuses, and resentment towards those that have it better in some way. The guy that makes you feel bad about your situation should be more sensible and stop being so successful, so that you don't feel inadequate about your personal circumstances and can safely avoid facing the truth and keep living as if everything was alright. Well it's not alright. There's a reason why we feel bad when we see someone that bests us in some regard. The competitive nature within us is telling us that they have it better, and that's unacceptable. So we are presented with two choices in order to fix this problem: one, we can cry out "inequality" and demand safe spaces where we don't have to meet these, oh so cruel, people, that make our flaws stand out for everyone to see, where we can avoid being challenged in any way, where we can stay comfortably until someday the real world slaps us across the face, and wakes us up to the harsh reality that the world is not a damn safe space. Or we can take the other path, the one less traveled, and the one that is rough and hard, and where even the strongest people get pushed to their emotional, mental, and physical limit. The one that tells you that if someone has it better then instead of complaining about it you should shut up and work as hard as you can to reach their level of success and use the fact that they are better than you in something as inspiration and not as an insult. So why would anyone take that path? Who could possibly want to recognize his shortcomings? Only those willing to take some hits and to accept negative feelings as part of the natural essence of existence will choose to go down the second path, because those are the ones that are able to recognize that growth comes only from experiencing some form of suffering, and are thus forced to reject the utopian fantasy in which no one's feelings are ever hurt and where everything negative is eradicated from the world. This is not the reality of existence, and there is not one single being on this earth that doesn't know this with absolute certainty either consciously or unconsciously. The way forward is to embrace suffering and challenges as tests of our will and of our strength, as obstacles to be overcome in the pursuit of greatness, as the shaping forces of excellence, and ultimately, of happiness. Because there is not a more unfulfilling life than that one in which resistance is never encountered, in which our capacity to persevere and fight isn't ever tested. I can't imagine how incredibly dull, boring and sad the world would become, were we to accept and embrace the growing culture that establishes victimhood as the ultimate form of bravery, rejecting and frowning upon actual bravery, actual merits and actual accomplishment. The circumstances of such a world would be absolutely catastrophic. Rejection of this victim culture means accepting responsibility, strength and discipline as some of the most respectable values of the human character, for they would not be seen as something to be eradicated to save us from feelings of inadequacy but rather as ideals to motivate us to be better and stronger.

This poisonous culture fueled by media and acceptance movements has us thinking from a very young age that all competition, all comparisons, and all disparities are a thing of evil. Participation trophies, children sport competitions in which scores aren't kept and where "everyone is a winner" may seem like a good thing, but in reality those types of things are exactly what are causing many members of my own and younger generations to be entitled, weak, irresponsible and resentful of everyone who has it better than them. Screeching millennials proclaim their unconformity with the status quo, demanding things from their parents, the government, the world, the universe; pointing fingers and calling whoever doesn't agree with their entitled worldview all kinds of names that will make their public reputation suffer, all of this while avoiding any type of responsibility, because that would mean taking control of their own life, and it is way more comfortable, at least in appearance, simply to blame others for the bad and take credit for the good.

I am not so blind as to not recognize that the circumstances that shape each person's life differ vastly from one human being to the other, but this is in no way, shape or form a valid excuse for not trying to improve those same circumstances, for the sake of our own well-being and the well-being of those closest to us.

It is imperative that we recognize the objectiveness of certain aspects—strength is better than weakness, discipline is better than laziness, being financially able is better than not being financially able. None of these things define the morality and the intrinsic "goodness" of a person, but they are factors that when objectively analyzed can be categorized as either good or bad. However much society tries to convince us that absolutely everything is subjective to the individual's perception, thus trying to validate wrong and false opinions, this isn't the way things are, and this is evident to anyone that dares defy the constant stream of false information fed to us by news outlets and social media.

The elimination of such objective criteria would have dire consequences, because the mere existence of concepts of good and bad define a blueprint towards which every human can strive. But who defines these concepts? Who decides whether something is good or bad? These are difficult questions. There are many external influences that can be of help when trying to come up with the answers: religion, culture or family values are normally those that tell us which forms of behavior are adequate and which ones aren't, but the real objective truth comes from deep within us, as most of the time we all know subconsciously what is right and what is wrong, and we also know what values are good and what behaviors are bad. It's a combination then, of external and internal factors that shape the scale of good and bad of every person. The important thing is to recognize that this scale exists and that not everything is subjective to personal perception.

Why are we on this earth, other than to grow, to achieve, to be great, however we choose to define greatness? What other purpose than this could there be for our very existence? I think we all know this but are too scared to act, to improve, to defy the odds, to challenge our limitations, to face obstacles with a relentless and stubbornly mindless mindset, to say "fuck it" and going for it.

The following chapters contain my thoughts on various virtues which I think any person should strive for, virtues that have been largely lost and forgotten in the modern world, and that are an essential aspect of the search for purpose and for our way in this world.

Strength

"No man has the right to be an amateur in the matter of physical training. It is a shame for a man to grow old without seeing the beauty and strength of which his body is capable."
-Socrates

The morality of strength

It is not very common to see or hear the words "morality" and "strength" combined in the same sentence. It is also not very common to discuss strength at all in this day and age. We all seem to be very concerned with questions about morality and ethics, and not at all preoccupied with those that make us wonder what has happened to those times in which every type of strength was recognized as a valuable virtue. Maybe it's because strength is unnecessary nowadays, and we know that being ethical and nice is the only thing that we should focus on. Or maybe it's because we've realized that there is much more praise directed towards those that are "moral" and "socially conscious" than towards those that are evidently strong. And praise is a drug, more addictive than heroin. There is nothing wrong with being socially responsible, when it's sincere. And there is nothing wrong with receiving praise for that responsibility. But it is absolutely wrong to preach morals and virtues that do not include the pursuit of strength as a priority. Socrates said it well: it truly is disgraceful to waste the physical potential of our body, justifying this loss by proclaiming the uselessness of strength and an aesthetic body. The human body is the most advanced machine in the world, and you can build it to be something of awe inspiring strength and beauty. And you should.

We try to be smarter, we try to be richer, we try to be kinder, and we try to be better. Why have we forgotten trying to be stronger? Because it's hard, it's painful and it requires a lot of time and patience. Because we are convinced that the effort required to become strong doesn't justify the limited benefits that strength represents in modern society. Because we are no longer fighting for survival every day, and can thus avoid the hassle of trying not to be weak. But being strong is necessary, and it's right. It's much easier to tell ourselves that being strong has absolutely no benefits in our comfortable bubble, but that is a blatant lie and you know it. No one is so incredibly blind as to not see that being strong is better than being weak, and that such an obvious virtue should be sought after with vigorous determination.

Not only is it right, but it is our duty to do whatever it takes to achieve, through sacrifice, the virtue of strength. It is our duty to ourselves, or else there wouldn't be that voice inside of us, hidden deeper in some individuals than others, that tells us that at some point our strength will be the only thing able to keep us from harm. And that voice is absolutely right, because whether we want it or not we will be thrown into battle, not necessarily a physical battle, but a battle nonetheless, at some point in this ugly, devastating life, and in the middle of the chaos that ensues when the struggle for survival appears as the only thing that matters will those that sacrificed something for the sake of strength not only survive, but thrive and win, while those that convinced themselves that strength was a thing of the past and that we can be protected from everything evil and hard by complaining hard enough will be beaten down by life. We owe this to ourselves, and to those we love and love us. Strength is morally right. It is the fulfillment of our duty as sons and daughters, parents and siblings, to be a lighthouse, standing tall and proud against the winds of despair that will break down everyone and anyone that hasn't recognized the value of strength and has shielded themselves in the comforts of modernity. It is our duty to be the voice of tranquility and order, to motivate and inspire through the strength of our bodies and our characters, to be a positive force. Strong is the moral thing to be.

The practicality of strength

It truly is disgraceful to let our physical potential remain undiscovered, to justify this shameful waste by proclaiming strength to be unnecessary, and time devoted to this purpose, therefore, a waste of time. Strength is our duty, a duty accepted by few but silently known by everyone. This becomes particularly evident on those occasions when encountering someone stronger makes us feel somehow inadequate.

In practical terms, strength is useful for preventing conflicts from escalating and for being able to defend yourself and your people when a conflict does escalate. Even the ones that fight the hardest to convince themselves and everyone else that strength has no practical use will look for a strong, competent man to protect them when shit goes down. And it will go down. In one way or another. And when that occurs will those that smugly brush strength off as a banal and basic characteristic, fit only for "meatheads", realize the wrong in their ways, while they look for someone to protect them with the strength they themselves don't have. It is not wise to wait for that to happen to realize the obvious importance of physical strength. It is much better to start giving it the importance it deserves and start working towards becoming an effective defender and protector of yourself and your family before you are actually required to rely on it.

How much can you take?

How strong is your back? How heavy your burden? Could it be heavier? Could you carry a little bit more? Could you take another step, and then another, while the weight pressing down on your shoulders gets heavier and heavier with each step? When you get beaten down mentally and physically, will you get up again and again or will you stop and quit and settle?

Will you keep quiet while everyone else around you is complaining about trivial problems and short-term preoccupations, and proudly walk upright with the weight of your goals and expectations firmly laid down on your back? If your dreams and goals are hard, so should you. How else are you going to take every disappointment, failure, doubt and damage coming your way? You become stubborn, you become hard, and you become strong. You don't whine and complain, you don't *demand* anything from anyone else and you definitely don't accept any type of weakness as a defining factor of yours.

Whatever life throws at you, take it on the chin. Men have grown from even the most devastating of events and circumstances, and that is the greatest achievement of the spirit of man. The fact that strong men can lose everything, can suffer immeasurably, and still come back from the edge of insanity and make the forces of life submit to their will could not be more inspiring. We should be ashamed of ourselves when we let small failures and ugly words divert us from the path that we so desperately want to follow. We should be mad at ourselves when we let weakness take the wheel and drive us down into a state of self-pity and victimhood. How can we possibly mutter sounds of complaint when there are people that use much greater suffering as a stepping stone towards greatness? Man was built to resist, to endure, to push back against anything and everything that tries to keep him from developing into a forceful and unstoppable machine, man was meant to proudly declare "I can take this, and everything that anyone may throw at me", for that is the purpose of anyone who walks this earth, to find those limits where spirits are broken and where we can, therefore, rebuild them into something even greater than before. Those are the men that move mountains with their will; they are the ones that feel inspired and not attacked by greatness and beauty, the ones that will never accept victimhood as a valid way of life. For man was never meant to be a victim, but rather to be strong, to be self-sufficient, proud and driven towards strength and greatness. So when the world tramples you down time and time again, get up and wipe the blood off your mouth, so you can spit in the face of evil and despair and push back with a force only known to those who have been knocked down and gotten up, those that have dedicated their lives to the pursuit of strength.

Heroism

Modern life leaves not a lot of room for people to be heroic. In the comings and goings of everyday life, not many things allow for true fulfillment. Normal, boring jobs, traffic, processed food. There is not much heroism in that kind of life. And it's no one's fault. It's just what we call progress. And of course it's true that we have progressed a lot from the times when every day was a struggle for survival. We can now be comfortable and quiet, and not worry about dying at any given second. That's good. But we have also lost some things along the way.

We have lost the opportunities for heroism. There is no sacrifice, there is no enemy to beat, and there is no great adversity to be overcome. Unless we willingly reject comfort and get out into the unknown to pursue something worthy.

If a "normal" life won't give us the challenges that our inner warrior so desperately craves, then we have to be smart (and a little bit dumb) and disregard the comforts of the modern world in order to find meaning and fulfillment through the small hurdles that we can introduce in our own way. Don't get too comfortable, make yourself work hard, force yourself to experience discomfort, challenge yourself as much as you can, and there will never be a situation that will break you, because you would've been preparing all your life for it. You can be the person that looks at that massive challenge and steps up when everyone else runs from it, you can be the one that overcomes, that grows, that pushes forward, but it will require enough guts to throw comfort into the trash can and put yourself out there, and start becoming someone that finds happiness and fulfillment in adversity itself. For you will start to look at adversity not as something that you have to avoid, but as something that will beat you down so that you can get back up and prove your steel over and over again. There is no better feeling in the world, and if you welcome adversity as something that will make you grow, there is not a single thing in this world that can beat you.

Mental strength

Of course physical strength is not the only important aspect of a strong person and a strong character. Strength transcends the physical realm, as it is also a feature that can be achieved within the mind. We all know this, but it is important to say it explicitly so as not to allow for any confusion.

The reason this section is part of this chapter, and not of any of the following ones, is that there is an undeniable link between physical and mental strength. It's rare to see someone have one type of strength and not the other, as the pursuit of strength in the physical sense will have the side effect of making you a much more determined and disciplined person, both aspects related to mental strength. Even if your goal has nothing to do with anything physical, working to become stronger physically is still something you should seek, even if only for the mental benefits that come with it. Being physically strong is your safety net, it's a virtue that will undoubtedly make you more confident, more assertive, and more disciplined, because unless you commit to hard work, you will never achieve the strength you desire, and even if you do, the only way to maintain it is through hard, constant effort.

Whenever you have doubts about the value of investing effort into the pursuit of strength, remember that the benefits of making this a priority will affect every single area of your life in a positive way, because there is not a single downside to being strong, and don't you ever let anyone convince you of the contrary. Having a strong body and a strong mind will bring you peace and security, it will make you a more honest person, as you're free of the insecurities that many times lead us to taking false steps and making wrong decisions, and it will be the trait that allows you to choose your path as you see fit, because you won't be constantly thinking about other people and putting them before yourself. Do whatever you can to develop this kind of fortitude and you'll not be manipulated again; you'll be able to be completely honest with yourself and with your goals and you will find peace and comfort in knowing your own power.

Life is a battleground

No matter how much we try to sugarcoat it, no matter how much progress we seem to make, no matter how much evil gets eradicated from the world, no matter how much people preach peace and love, the world has always and will forever be a battleground, a ruthless place where only the strongest get what they want, and everyone else is left wondering how it's possible for them to be unhappy and unsuccessful, when we were told for a long time that everyone was deserving and that everyone was a winner. It's sad, and yet, sobering, to realize that even if we roar mightily to the skies, the world will never consist of equality, that regardless of how much we try to create an earth where everyone can be happy and feel good all the time, competition will always exist and some will be rewarded more than others, some will be happier than others, more successful, and also, better than others.

Competition doesn't necessarily happen between two or more individuals, and competition doesn't mean that the only way to win is to beat and bury someone else who's also trying to rise. Competition takes place every day, and every instance of competition is a fight in which your abilities to push back are tested. We are always competing: against ourselves, against our past, against our temptations and bad habits, against those that want to see us fail, against life itself. Competition is a basic truth that will always govern many of our endeavors and interactions, and guess what? The strong always have a better chance of winning than the weak.

Such is the way things are and a quick, logical analysis would inevitably yield the fact that we have to train and prepare ourselves for the perpetual battles of life by pursuing strength. This isn't a pretty and delicate task, nor should it be. It's a gruesome and challenging path to follow.

Treating your workout sessions and the hours spent on the church of iron as merely a means to look "fit", or as a social opportunity to chat and feel good is both a waste of time and a perpetuation of a culture that is too focused on faking stuff and forgets that noble achievements don't usually happen as a consequence of something pretty and soft, but as a result of ugly, sweaty, and gruesome action.

Omission of the previous statements is what has made of the gym a place where most people go to chat or simply to be able to proudly make claims about their "fit" lifestyle and the values of their character. We are slowly creeping away from those times in which people at the gym would be actually working hard and suffering physical pain for the sake of improvement, and into a soft age where the gym is packed with people that use gloves because "calluses look ugly", that use pussy pads for squats because "the iron bar feels uncomfortable", that simply look at their phone for an hour and then leave. Treat your time at the gym as a sacred ritual, see it as a means to test your will and become resilient. Throw excuses out of the window, throw complaints out of the window, and find meaning in the voluntary hardships that are to be found when you train. It hurts? Good. Are your hands getting rougher? Good. They are reminders of your hard work. Be proud of those things that prove that you've put in the work, don't try to avoid them, don't try to exchange them for what you think other people will like, and make of them a constant reminder that you're made of stronger metal, that you've dedicated hour upon hour to the pursuit of improving your physical capabilities.

Synthesis

Strength is not, by any means, unnecessary, nor is it a thing of the past. It is not superficial to worry about your body, and strength is not merely a physical attribute. The pursuit of strength is one of the most fulfilling quests any person can engage in, and you should consider it your duty to make of this search a priority, for deep inside every one of us there is an undeniable feeling, telling us that we weren't born to let our physical potential go to waste, that we were meant to always strive for greater strength.

Strength is also very practical, regardless of the contrary claims made by weak people. You can choose to be blind and ignore all the signs and evidence that weakness is never a virtue, and that strength is always one, or you can stop listening to people who care nothing about you and start becoming what you were always meant to be: strong, powerful, determined and unstoppable.

Discipline

"We must all suffer one of two things: the pain of discipline or the pain of regret or disappointment."
-Jim Rohn

"I don't feel like it"

We all have responsibilities and duties, and guess what? Absolutely no one enjoys every activity and task that their daily life demands of them. Besides, it's much easier to simply lie on the couch and eat potato chips while convincing yourself that you'll do whatever you need to do tomorrow, or that you'll find a way to work around it and not do that boring thing at all. We have become way too used to this type of mentality. It makes you wonder what kind of weak society we live in when most people can't even follow a workout routine for more than a month. And no, it's not for lack of time, so save that excuse for someone else and stop lying to yourself. It's also not because you don't enjoy it, or because you don't think it is useful. It's because you don't have the discipline, and as I said, it's because you're making excuses and brainwashing yourself into thinking that you are doing the right thing by being lazy. And going to the gym is just a basic example, and it may or may not apply to your own life. It doesn't matter. The point is that we could all be more disciplined, and should therefore wake up, stop making excuses, and do what needs to be done, no matter how tired we may be.

Discipline is probably the one thing we, as young people in a weak-minded society, lack the most. We know what we have to do (most of the time), we know what we want, we know the steps that we have to take (or at least we know what NOT to do), and yet we don't seem to have enough strength and willpower to withdraw from binge watching Netflix and go get what we want.

If you don't "feel like it", that's an even better

reason to go do it. You don't want to study? Do it. You don't feel like going out to the gym in the middle of winter? Put your boots and jacket on and go lift some heavy weights. There is nothing to be won from doing those things when you want to. That's easy. Growth happens when you learn to do them when you DON'T want to, when you have to overcome your own feeble mind and the excuses that it so conveniently presents. You don't feel like it? Good. Go do it. That's when discipline starts to develop, and it feels great to be able to control your mind and not let excuses keep you from acting. Consider it a challenge: next time you're being lazy and procrastinating, remember this section, get up as quickly as possible and go do something productive. Then quietly congratulate yourself, for you've won that little battle. Those little battles will add up, if you keep challenging yourself, and you'll be able to win the truly important battles of life.

Your excuses are not valid

No. Not even that one. Nor that other one. I don't care if you're tired, I don't care if you're sad, I don't care if you don't "have the time". Neither should you. Ask yourself: Is this thing that I don't want to do important for myself and my future? If the answer is yes (which it probably is, otherwise you wouldn't even be thinking about it), then know that no excuse is valid. None. Think about that the next time you want to quit or avoid your responsibilities. Remember that you could've paid your dues. And you chose not to. Know consciously that you chose not to, because that excuse or that justification means nothing. The fact is that you had something to do and you didn't do it. Unless there was an extreme circumstance (which there probably wasn't), you just avoided your duties because you were lazy. If you feel bad about that, then good. Because you know what? You won't want to feel like that again, so hopefully next time you'll remember that you felt lazy and undisciplined and bad and won't want to feel like that again, so you'll be more responsible and go do what you have to do. Feeling bad can be a good thing, as it forces us to find the strength to change our behavior. It is through feeling bad that we have the opportunity to change. It is by forcing ourselves to realize the wrong in our ways that we can grow. It is necessary to feel bad so we can rise, and learn. Excuses will get you nowhere, and they will even beat you down, for they are but a manifestation of our lack of willpower. Remember that the next time you're making excuses, and you'll never feel comfortable avoiding your duties again. And that's a good thing, because you'll do better next time.

Respect discipline

No one enjoys feeling lazy and lethargic. Therefore, we tend to make up a million excuses that justify our lack of forward momentum, convincing ourselves that those things that we are too scared to do don't really matter, that those things that we want aren't really that important to us. We make huge intellectual efforts in order to go around the fact that the things we desire with all our strength (material and otherwise) will not come unless we stop justifying our inaptitude to quit our lousy habits and start working hard towards those things that really matter.

Precisely because of this, we tend to criticize those that do have that discipline. We do this because we need to find a way to not feel bad, and when someone possessing the qualities that we desire most ourselves (such as discipline) appears before us, it is a natural reaction to feel inadequate, for in that moment our flaws become evident. That person is telling us: "Look at me, I'm doing what you could be doing but are too weak to do". Man, that doesn't feel good. But not feeling good is the perfect indicator that we should change something. We can face this as men, taking it all in and realizing that we have to make the effort in order to advance, or we can face it like cowards, and go into our little bubble of confirmation where we can comfortably live surrounded by the lies that tell us that living carelessly and recklessly is the best way to live, because we are "having fun". "Fun" isn't even that important. I can't even tell you how many times people have justified their reckless lifestyle by proclaiming youth's obligation to have "fun" at all costs. I'm sure you've heard that a million times as well. Go have fun after you've made something worthy of yourself, go have fun after you can actually claim to have paid your dues. Fun is feeble and doesn't last very long. Pursue happiness, pursue greatness, pursue success, pursue discipline, pursue honor. Those are the things that are worthwhile, and if, for their sake, we have to sacrifice some immediate "fun", it is absolutely worth it.

We have to learn to respect those people that are determined and disciplined. We can and should draw inspiration from them, as an ideal to work towards. We have to stop calling people "boring" or "self-absorbed", when they have managed to sacrifice the easy pleasures of today's society in favor of a life of struggle, growth and the pursuit of greatness.

Discipline=Freedom

I'm writing this section shortly after watching a Jocko Willink video called "Discipline=Freedom", so credits to him. Jocko Willink, for those who don't know, is a Navy SEAL, author and podcaster, who talks about discipline, motivation and responsibility. I recommend that you check out his podcast, and also his books.

It's counterintuitive to think that discipline could be related to freedom, as we tend to think that freedom is simply the absence of responsibility, and we usually equate it to living a life with no worries, no goals, and no structure. That's why this principle seemed so appealing to me. Can it be that freedom and discipline are directly correlated?

Discipline is not a way for you to tyrannize yourself, discipline is not about some sort of coercion that controls your every day and keeps you from being free. It's quite the opposite, actually. Discipline is how you will free yourself from the actual coercive power of your own bad habits, of your laziness, of your lack of willpower. Discipline is the ultimate goal, because discipline is the only way to actually get things done. Motivation will not make you stand up in the morning and work for a better future, because motivation is fleeting, and inconsistent. When every cell in your body is telling you to stop, motivation, faith, or anything else, won't be enough to push you forward. You need extreme discipline for that. When you are experiencing defeat, when you are feeling down, when you only want to climb into bed and feel sorry for yourself, the only thing that will save you is discipline.

In that sense, discipline suddenly becomes the path to freedom, for it keeps you from being a victim of circumstances and emotions, and enables you to take control of your own life and to decide what is important, and it allows you to execute and accomplish, because if you have enough discipline, no amount of excuses, failures, pain or despair will be enough to divert you from the path that you want to follow. Discipline is the only way to overcome your weaknesses, and live a life in which you have the power to decide what you want to do every day, and who you want to be.

Synthesis

The path to any worthy achievement is full of distractions and reasons to stray away from it, it is full of hardships and it requires constant effort, for at every step of the way you'll be tempted to quit. The only thing that will help you fight those feelings and keep those distractions at bay is discipline.

Discipline is your path to freedom, the path to the life you want and the only thing that will make you be constantly improving. Motivation wavers, your environment changes, your circumstances change, and your energy levels change, so make of discipline the one thing that is constant in your life.

Toughness

"You show me anybody that's great in anything they do, I'll show you somebody that's persevered, demonstrated that mental toughness to overcome some obstacles and adversity."
-Sean Mcvay

The reality of life

The world is full of suffering, full of despair and devastation, full of death and pain. It's a harsh world we live in. And we will get eaten up if we don't arm ourselves to face the relentless pressure that is essential to life. I know this may be hard to accept, as nowadays we are constantly being told that mankind is inherently good, that we should always see the good in people, that we shouldn't judge anyone before we "know" them well enough. And while it's true that some people are inherently good and have your best interests at heart, many people do not. And if you believe all the feel-good nonsense that we are constantly being fed and choose to go naively through life, you will be taken advantage of, and you'll be an easy target for those that want to harm you. What I'm saying is: be wary. Be wary, because the world is full of snakes that want to use you for their advantage, be wary of hypocrites and people that tell you whatever you want to hear. Beware of this world, for it's a harsh place. Don't think even for a second that the struggle for survival has ended. Remember that even in our modern, "safe", world, every day is still a struggle for survival. The people that know this are the ones that are able to develop the hardest shells, and face and endure the harshest of situations without breaking down. Even though it's clear that we live much more safely now than we did many years ago, evil still exists, and it's therefore necessary, now more than ever, so as not to be an easy prey for those forces that seek to harm you. These "forces" are not necessarily evil people, and are not necessarily evil things per se, but they may simply be difficult or sad situations that will affect you much more if you are not mentally ready for them.

Suffering, death, difficult financial times for you and your family, loneliness, or any other negative situation you may think of, will undoubtedly appear at some point in your life. Nobody can escape that. For that reason it is very wise to know this as an undeniable truth, and use the time before such a tragedy happens to become someone that will not be put down by suffering, and you do that by training your mind to accept discomfort, and by constantly working not to let small, stressful situations have an effect on your emotional state and overall well-being. This is how you can then be ready for when the big challenges of life try to trip you over, otherwise they will beat you down and make you suffer a whole lot more.

The hardest struggle happens within

We live in an era in which most of the outside, physical threats have been eradicated, or at least controlled to a high degree. And that has allowed us to be less concerned with physical struggles for survival and more concerned with questions about the spirit and morality of mankind. As I've already said, the world is a harsh place, but most of us don't have to worry constantly about physical survival all the time, which leaves a lot of free time for us to discover new trouble inside our minds.

Most of us are quite aware of what I'm talking about here, as it is quite common to experience the difficult situation of trying to control your mind and your thoughts. It's quite funny that one of the most difficult tasks we face is keeping our minds from turning against us. But that is still a very real and very difficult task. It is imperative that we somehow manage to make our mind work for us, and not against us, for there will be times when all of our will and determination will be tested, and staying sane, and on the right path will depend on having our mind on our side.

There are already enough people trying to convince you that you are not worthy, that you are not good enough, so you desperately need your thoughts to be supportive of you, otherwise you will start to believe all that negativity. Become your biggest fan, and train your mind to be a refuge, where you can find peace and comfort when things are not going your way, instead of breaking down completely.

That is the inner struggle that each one of us must face: the fight against our own negativity, against our own feeling of grief, of sadness, against the weakness within that tells us that we should give up, that we can take no more, that we should retreat to the easy path and forget about trying to become someone worthy of the greatest success, the greatest happiness and the most rewarding life possible. Controlling your runaway thoughts, especially at those times when they may seem justified, is not easy, but it is a necessity for your well-being that you make a conscious effort to have your mind work for you, and not against you. This requires a sort of overconfident stubbornness, for it will sometimes mean ignoring other people's opinions about you. Do not, however, confuse this heightened confidence with arrogance, because I'm not talking about ignoring everything and never accepting that we are wrong. I'm stating the fact that most people don't care enough about you to know what's best for you, and therefore you should know that it is not mandatory for you to heed to their advice. Listen to them, openly and critically analyze what it is they're saying, and decide on your own whether or not that advice is something that you want to follow.

Learn, work to have your mind be a positive force, and make sure that you are doing what is best for you, your dreams, and the future you want to create. That is the inner struggle of our lives, not to let ourselves be strayed from the path that we know in our hearts is right for us, not to let our spirit be killed by insults or criticism, to be absolutely sure that we are doing what's best for us, while at the same time having enough humility to recognize when we have done something wrong. It is a difficult job, and one that will never be fully completed, for our minds will have their moments of fragility in which they push us down instead of lifting us up, but the true goal is to minimize those instances and manage to find peace inside our minds and outside in the world.

It's in your nature

The good thing about all of this is that we are perfectly built to endure, and thrive, in tough, difficult places such as our world. Think about it: throughout all of history, since the very first moment that the earth started existing, for every creature, including human beings, every single minute was a struggle for survival. The world has never been a kind place, and because we are the result of millions of years of evolution, we are literally built to survive. Our nature is the nature of a tough creature, capable of fighting, of carrying its own weight, capable of surviving in even the most desolate environments. Remember that when you start to let bad words hurt your feelings. Remember that you are living in the most comfortable and soft era that has ever existed, and you are whining because you cannot even bear the most petty of discomforts.

Never forget that you are the result of endless years of evolution, made to be relentless and unstoppable, made to be the complete opposite of a victim (and the opposite of being a victim is NOT being an oppressor), you have, as a human, all the qualities necessary to persist and be successful in harsh environments. We are made to suffer, so that we can grow from that suffering.

Train yourself to endure, to resist

In a world that is constantly becoming more and more comfortable, and where the normal thing to do is to seek a way to surround ourselves with bubble wrap in order to avoid any and all things that can make us upset somehow, the only way forward is consciously acknowledging that without some discomfort there is no motivation, and no reason to grow, thus recognizing that in order to become better, to become great, we must put ourselves in uncomfortable situations, purposefully introducing them into our daily routines so that our bodies and our minds can grow used to discomfort. For the real world is full of discomfort, and trying to convince ourselves that we can somehow dodge and avoid every single thing that will make us feel uneasy is a naïve and childish thing to do. And we are not children anymore. The only way to be ready for all the difficulties that we will undoubtedly encounter is to reject comfort as a definitive state, and use comfortable times as training grounds in which our minds can become stronger, by putting ourselves in adversity's way and facing it head on. Just imagine how badly the world would beat you up if the first challenge you ever encountered was a big one. Just imagine how unbearable the pain would be if you worked all your life to shield yourself from suffering and then had to face some gruesome, devastating situation with your mind and your spirit unaccustomed to adversity. I think that prospect is enough reason to try and learn how to act in the face of adversity, to make a conscious effort to become comfortable in discomforting times, so that you'll be ready to overcome every challenge that may appear in front of you.

"Expressing your feelings"

We have all heard people preach about how strong and courageous one is if one is able to "express" their feelings. We have been told that it's okay to cry if you feel sad, that it's okay to let go and let yourself be controlled by your emotions. Anyone who tries to have a different opinion, and who regards the uncontrolled expression of emotions as a mostly negative action will be shunned and shamed (believe me, I've tried). "We shouldn't teach young men not to cry" is the most common representation of what I'm talking about. And yet, we never ask why we shouldn't. We just eat that up as a wise commandment and move on, repeating it only when someone is either trying not to cry or feels bad for having let sadness beat him.

I don't think that is a smart thing to believe. There is a reason why we have the capacity for rational thought. It is precisely because of this exclusively human characteristic that we can and should learn to govern our emotions instead of letting them govern us. Why on earth are we claiming so surely that expressing feelings and emotions is such a good thing? How many times have you actually done that and gotten a positive result because of it? The occasions in which any good comes from crying or getting angry or letting our emotions take the wheel are extremely limited, if there are any.

Most of the time, our emotions are biased, and thus not exactly in line with the correct course of action, and yet we still think that it's "the right choice" to "follow your heart". Well, I don't buy that. Follow your head instead. When your feelings contradict your rational thoughts, which is most of the time, the smart—and also the more difficult—decision is to make a choice while being devoid of the influence of emotion. Controlling your emotions is hard, but it's good, and it is, no matter how much we try to deny it, something that does indeed demonstrate the strength of a person's mind. Now, this doesn't mean that we should do away with all empathy and sympathy, or that everyone who expresses feelings is weak and worthless. It also doesn't mean that we should become machines and ignore all feelings and emotions. What it means is that preaching the expression of feelings as an inherently good and right course of action is of no benefit to anyone, because there are many instances in which we can and should choose not to show our feelings so directly, and where stopping for a second to recognize this rationally, will help us act in a way that will indeed be beneficial to us.

Also, there is no dishonesty in choosing not to act on your feelings. On the contrary, being able to control your impulses in favor of the actions that will get you closer to your goals is a demonstration of your unwavering honesty with yourself and your values.

Synthesis

There is no way to escape the horrors of the world. Sooner or later everyone will encounter suffering and despair, and this is an unavoidable fact of life for everyone. Due to this absolute truth, it is up to us to prepare and to learn how to endure and how to face this suffering, and this, as everything else, requires practice. This learning process begins with stuff as simple as making yourself uncomfortable, learning to control your mind and your emotions, voluntarily facing some kind of pain and confronting your weaknesses head-on, instead of shying away from every challenge and crying out for protection from someone else.

Remember that your nature as a human being is to thrive in difficult environments, to adapt even to the most devastating circumstances, and you'll find within you a strength previously unknown to you, a strength that'll make you able to take the biggest hits and rise victorious from the depths of pain and suffering.

Force yourself to be tough, when you're down and sad, when you feel like everything is falling apart, make of your mind your best friend and shield yourself with the knowledge that you will endure whatever you're going through, that you'll wake up a stronger man, and that you'll use rock bottom as a place where your own power and your own ability to keep going in even the toughest of circumstances can be tested and proven.

Responsibility

The past doesn't define you

I fully understand the fact that there are things that happen to us, that have happened to us, that have a long lasting effect in the way we experience everyday life, in the way we act and in the way we think. It is quite obvious that our upbringing, our childhood, our earliest memories get stuck in our subconscious and determine many things about how we'll behave in the future. We are all, in some way, products of our past. We are not however, ONLY products of our past. That is a key distinction, because it's important to recognize that while the things we have experienced have partly given shape to our personality, we are also capable of changing that personality, we are also able to reject the common consensus that what we are today is exclusively and unalterably a consequence of what we have experienced in the past.

We are much better than that. Our past suffering, while possibly tragic, determines our life today only if we allow it. We shouldn't think that it's okay to be slaves of our past. It is common to accept former circumstances and past experiences as a valid reason for people not to be the best they could be, but we need to realize that the past is gone, and it can grip us no more unless we keep using it to justify our present.

Whatever tragedy we may have experienced, whatever things have hurt us in the past are not the reason why we aren't where we want to be. They may be part of the reason, they may have made our way a little bit harder, but none of those things that happened are responsible for our circumstances now, today.

The fact of the matter is this: you, as a human being, have the magnificent ability to choose your own actions, thus choosing and defining your own life. Every moment, you have the capacity to think consciously about what you are going to do next, and it is up to you to let your past determine those actions or not. It's a hard thing to do, because if you accept this, then suddenly you become the one factor that determines what your life looks like, how it develops, which in turn makes it impossible to point fingers at other people or at other situations and blame them for your circumstances. Remember that you can always choose not to be defined by anything else but your goals, dreams and ambitions, and that not even the most tragic of pasts can keep you from doing what you want to do. Only you can do that. We are stronger than our past, we are stronger than our suffering, and each and every one of us can choose to grow and not be weighed down by anything, ever.

No one else is responsible for your situation

Just as no previous experience can determine your situation today, no other person or entity is to blame for whatever happens in your life. Your parents are not to blame, society is not to blame, your teacher, your friends, your girlfriend, are also not to blame. Pointing fingers is a representation of weakness and fragility, something that we do to avoid hurting our ego, so that we can continue living in a fake world where everything bad can be attributed to someone else. We can't become someone that tries to escape the reality of their lack of discipline, willpower, or character by cowardly pointing to someone else. That will get us nowhere. I think you know that what I'm saying is true. It makes all the sense in the world, doesn't it? I know it's not what we've been told, or how we see most people act, for the social norm nowadays is to be whiny and irresponsible, and never take ownership for anything. The world needs more people that reject this convention of complaints and finger-pointing, the world needs young people that step up when things happen and say "I'm responsible for this, and I'm going to fix this". Note that being responsible for your situation doesn't mean feeling guilty when something bad happens, and satisfied when something good does; being responsible means being able to look at every situation with a critical eye that allows you to identify what you could've done differently. I'm talking about being a problem solver, and in order to become that it's absolutely mandatory to become responsible first.

If we are always blaming someone else then we will convince ourselves that there's nothing that we could've done to prevent a certain situation, which in turn will mean that there is no reason for us to try to fix it, and therefore no motivation to get better. That's why it's important to take ownership for absolutely everything that occurs in your life. It will be like unlocking a secret part of your brain that instantly allows you to look for solutions instead of simply brushing off every hurdle and difficult situation as someone else's fault and responsibility.

Freedom

Imagine for a second that you could choose every single detail about your life. Imagine that you could choose what car you'd drive, what house you'd live in, your family, what your social life would look like, how you would look and feel, what things you'd do in your free time, where you'd work, etc. Imagine that it was as simple as selecting items from a catalogue. Wouldn't that be sensational?

That is not a crazy dream. That's what happens when you take ownership for every single detail of your life. That's a simplified way of representing the process that takes place once your mind becomes accustomed to the new way of improved living that is derived from becoming the sole determinant of where your life goes. Because we are conscious, smart creatures, we are able to think long-term and plan ahead. So if there is some desire within us, we can create an action plan around that goal, thus making sure that every action that we take gets us closer to that ending point. This is not easy, and it takes practice, but it is absolutely possible. What usually happens and what most people normally do is the following: they have a goal or a dream and don't realize that anything that has any worth will not come easily and quickly, but will be incredibly difficult to obtain. We tend to underestimate how much work and time a worthy project will take. So we convince ourselves that by doing the bare minimum and thinking hard enough about it, our dream will materialize because we "deserve" it. And then, when it doesn't happen, we tend to do an absolutely gigantic effort to avoid feeling responsible for our lack of commitment and hard work towards the completion of our goal. That leads to us blaming it on some external factor, thus allowing our ego to feel satisfied, as it wasn't our fault at all. That's what most people do, but that's not going to get you anywhere.

The correct way to set goals and actually achieving them is as follows: you decide what it is you want, and then make a conscious decision to do everything in your power to achieve it. Then, you work as hard and as smart as you can, and if you somehow don't accomplish it in the timeframe that you set, you analyze what you could've done better and try again, until you make it. You take ownership, and you accept that you and your actions are the only ones responsible for your results. You take control over your decisions, and thus, over your life. You become the only one responsible for getting the things that you want and for determining the shape of your life. That's *true* freedom. That's what we are all looking for. Freedom is about taking back control over your own life. Freedom means that you are the one that determines who you are, what you do and how you behave. Freedom means that you are not at the mercy of anything or anyone, and that you are a conscious being that can literally decide what his life looks like.

Start changing those habits that do you no good, start working harder, becoming stronger, more driven, more motivated. Become a role model, become someone that other people can look up to and direct every single action of yours towards a mental image of how you want your life to be. Find yourself in growth, find comfort in the process and remember that true freedom is a possibility exclusive to humanity, for true freedom is the capacity to choose our feelings, our thoughts, our actions and our future.

Actions are all that matters

Ideas are usually glorified. Everything revolves around having ideas, good ideas preferably. If the idea is good, then our business will thrive. If the idea is good, then results will follow. This is completely and utterly false. This glorification of ideas has made us forget that ideas, by themselves, are worth nothing. Nothing at all. If I had an idea about how to cure cancer, would I be curing cancer? Of course not. If I managed to translate this idea into a physical object, then maybe I would. That's a pretty dumb and basic example, but it explains what I'm trying to say well enough. The only way for ideas to be worth anything is to make those ideas a tangible reality. I know this may seem obvious, but way too often we tend to let our minds simply wander and think about stuff, coming up with wonderful ideas that could be very valuable. But more often than not, that's where the process stops. We come up with some potentially world-changing concept and imagine how much that idea could help people, and then we do absolutely nothing else. This cycle repeats itself endlessly, and afterwards we are left with a thousand ideas in our mind but without a hint of anything tangible.

This can be attributed to a couple of different factors: first, the glorification of ideas naturally causes us to think that having an idea is "good enough", and that after coming up with a concept no further task is required to reap the benefits of a good idea. Second, procrastination and overall laziness makes us much more likely to engage in activities that don't require lots of effort, such as letting our mind wander, and much less likely to pull ourselves by our bootstraps and start taking real, tangible steps towards the development and realization of that idea. Third, because of the nature of the modern world, we are constantly becoming more and more fearful of failure, which directly causes us to be less likely to take risks (and pursuing any creation is definitely a risk, as it will require some time and money).

I think that the single most important difference between those that "make it" and those that don't is that the first group recognizes that every single valuable thing must be earned through action, through effort and sweat, while the second one has been misled into believing that all they have to do is think hard enough and results will somehow appear, forgetting that the only time thoughts are valuable is when they start directing our actions in the real, physical world.

It's also important to note that results come as a consequence of consistent practice, not as a result of hours upon hours of learning the theory of whatever it is that you want to accomplish. It's very easy to get caught up in the never-ending stream of theoretical information found online and never put anything into practice. Other than the reasons mentioned before, this is also due to the fact that precisely because it is so easy to find information about any topic nowadays, we delay actually performing in the real world, thinking that we must keep learning until we know the theory inside out and backwards. Even though there is nothing wrong with preparing oneself properly before embarking into a new venture, we mustn't forget that only knowing the theory about something is useless, unless we put that theory into practice. Remember that there is no use in learning all the theory unless it's accompanied by real action.

Recognizing that actions breed results—and therefore accepting that when something doesn't go the way we would have wanted it to go it's because of wrongly chosen actions—will drastically change the way we look at things, as it will allow us to reject any sort of entitlement that tells us that we should have something merely because we thought long and hard about it, or because we know everything there is to know about that topic.

Act, move forward, take steps towards your goal, learn by doing, become a man of action, not a man that knows everything but does nothing. Go get whatever it is you want to get through real effort, real challenges and real sweat. Become the creator of your own life, for you are the owner of your thoughts, which makes you the sole person responsible for your actions, your circumstances and your whole world.

Synthesis

It has been a very long time since we decided to focus on what our rights are, and have forgotten to understand and accept our responsibilities. It is now time to realize that our life's fate is not in someone else's hands, but exclusively in ours. No matter how hard your life has been, how much pain you've been through, or how much trouble you're currently in, always remember that you have the power to get out of that hole, and to change your life drastically. The power of a single human mind is unbelievable, when combined with purposeful action.

Do not fall into the trap of believing everything to be a basic right, do not go around thinking that you are deserving of everything for merely desiring it and happening to be alive. You get what you work for, and what you earn, and your life is a direct reflection of your actions, thoughts, and decisions.

We all come from different backgrounds, we have all had different experiences, which means that the way will be harder for some than for others, but the principle of absolute responsibility remains the same for everyone: even in the worst of circumstances, as Viktor Frankl so wisely wrote, "Everything can be taken from a man but one thing: the last of the human freedoms – to choose one's attitude in any given set of circumstances, to choose one's own way." Rejoice, because from now on you are free to choose your reactions, your emotions, your thoughts, your actions, your decisions. From this moment onward there is no outside force strong enough to stray you from your dreams. You are now the exclusive forger of your destiny, you are free to accomplish and grow, to learn and act, to execute and create, and to build the future in which you want to live.

Focus

"The direction of your focus is the direction your life will move. Let yourself move toward what is good, valuable, strong and true."

-Ralph Marston

Decide your path

As we grow older, the pressure to decide what we want to do and what we want our life to look like grows with us. It's a normal part of life to feel kind of lost in that period of time when we suddenly become (or are expected to be) responsible adults, capable of fending for ourselves and who should have a clear idea of who we are. When this isn't the case, as it is with most of us, the pressure becomes so big that we would rather turn on the auto-pilot and make it stop, instead of facing this pressure and start asking ourselves the tough questions that will determine which path we are to follow. It is imperative that we go through the trouble of suffering the uncertainty that comes when we have enough guts to face those questions, because otherwise we'll be lost for goodness knows how long. The problem with being lost is that you can willfully ignore the fact that you are lost only for some time, but you'll eventually realize that you have no idea of who you are or why you do what you do. You don't want this realization to come when it's too late, which is what happens with most people, and why midlife crises are so extremely common. This realization is but an epiphany that forces you to evaluate your whole life and every choice you've ever made, and most people realize that they know nothing about themselves, and notice too late that their ideal life is far different from the one they are actually living. The sooner we man up and look at ourselves critically, the sooner we ask ourselves those grueling questions, the clearer our path will become, and if we take the wheel now and start to decide how we want our life to be, we won't have to wait until we are forty to realize that we aren't completely satisfied with our current situation.

The first step towards the life that you so deeply desire is to stop running in circles for some time, and dedicate your whole energy towards understanding yourself, your dreams, your passions, your goals. How do you really want your life to be in ten years? How about in twenty? Do you want a family? What does it look like? Where will you live? What will you do for a living? Understand that it isn't necessary, and it's probably impossible, to suddenly know the answers to each one of those questions, but the important thing is to ask them. Asking yourself all of this will get your mind working, and the answers to those questions will blind sight you when you least expect them. But if you never even ask them there's no reason for your brain and your subconscious to try and find the answers.

Question your life, question what you've always seen as obvious, start asking deeper questions and you'll simultaneously start finding the path that you want to follow. That's the first step towards finding out the truth about yourself, and once you've begun to create a mental picture of your ideal life, you can start directing every action towards that goal. But you have to know what the goal is first, otherwise you'll just be drifting aimlessly and following everyone else that is also lost.

Act according to your end goal

Every action should have a purpose. Any endeavor should be directed towards something. There's no point, and no purpose, in acting out of emotion, or in acting for the sake of acting. Because most people have no idea of who they want to be in this world, they just act out of inertia, without thinking about why they do what they do. That's why it's of the utmost importance to do what I mentioned in the previous section, because without a clear definition of a goal there is no way that we can know how to act to achieve it.

I know this can seem kind of obvious, but think about how many times you act in a way that is counterproductive to your goals. We all do this. We waste our precious time doing things that are absolutely irrelevant, we spend our money in shit that isn't good for us in any way, we surround ourselves with fake people that push us down, we do a bunch of things that get us no closer to our ideal life, and we are left wondering why we are not where we want to be, when we have done absolutely nothing consistent with our goals. It's crazy how obvious it is, and yet most of the time we can't get our act together and start moving in the right direction. Call it social pressure, call it lack of guidance, or call it plain laziness, the fact of the matter is that we simply can't get off our asses and move forward. At least this is the case most of the time. And yet, more often than not we absolutely know what we should be doing, or at least we know what we should not be doing, so ignorance is a weak excuse.

The point is this: the only way to reach any goal and accomplish anything you want to accomplish is to direct every single action of every day towards that objective, and structure your life around that ambition. Of course you could half-ass everything and eventually accomplish what it is you want out of luck and taking thrice as long, but I'm pretty sure that what you want is not to be successful and happy when you are close to dying, but rather to get it as soon as possible to enjoy it for as long as you can. So start performing, start doing the things that will get you closer to your goal, prioritize them over everything else, and stop wasting your energy, your time, and your money on things that do not matter.

Establish priorities

It's hard to keep focused and to know what to do when we haven't established a clear hierarchy of wants, needs, goals and values. If there is no blueprint to guide us, the chances of drifting aimlessly and blindly go up exponentially. We've talked about asking ourselves deep, meaningful questions in order to find the path that will lead us towards happiness and success, by making our mind work on trying to decipher what we really want. Very much in line with that proposal, is the fact that establishing priorities is a fundamental exercise for getting where we want to get.

It's astonishing how crooked most people's priority scales are. I mean, most people complain constantly about their lives, or at least about some aspects of them, and yet they do absolutely nothing to fix those aspects. People complain about their finances, and would rather spend hundreds of dollars on alcohol and cigarettes instead of buying a goddamn personal finances book for twenty dollars. Try to sell a course of something useful, try to sell a book about productivity, try to provide people with useful information, try to make videos teaching something and you'll see what I'm talking about. People will refuse to watch a twenty minute video about something useful but will spend two hours watching some YouTuber talk about their first kiss. I mean what in hell? How do you come to decide that you want to spend your time like that? People will not buy a book for fifteen dollars, deeming it "too expensive" or "out of their budget", but will not hesitate to waste 50 dollars (minimum) going out simply because it's the social norm. And then they are left wondering where all their money went. Well instead of throwing it down the drain you could've at least invested in knowledge of some kind, or you could've not gone out and put that money to better use.

I know that I am somewhat ranting here, and some people may think that I'm getting on the moral high horse and claiming that I always spend my time and money correctly. Obviously I'm not saying that, as I most definitely am not exempt from occasionally misusing my time and money. But I'm working on reducing those mistakes. And damn, even if I make the same mistakes, the fact of the matter remains the same. It's wrong not to have a clearly defined hierarchy of priorities, and that will always be the case. Not knowing what's important and what's not, or even worse, ignoring what you know to be important in favor of idle pleasures and fleeting "fun", is the surest way to a hollow and deeply unhappy life. It is not enough to vaguely state which values and which things are important to you. It's essential to turn them into a definite and clear ladder of virtues, values, and overall priorities, and also to let that structure of priorities actually guide your decisions. Consciously ignoring your value structure is one of the easiest ways of feeling unhappy, because you'd be acting against something that you decided is important for you and weren't disciplined enough to follow through with the priorities that you decided were adequate for yourself.

I encourage you to be consistent with your inner structure of values and priorities, otherwise you'll consciously be acting against your interests and against your better judgement, and that's never a good thing. Ignore everything that strays you away from your goals, focus on the things that matter, use your time and money wisely, and the things you want will come.

Confidently stubborn

Stubbornness is usually described as a character flaw, and in many cases it is. It's not good to be arrogantly stubborn, believing that you know more than everyone else and that no one can tell you anything, because you already know it. That's definitely a flaw, as it will be impossible for anyone who thinks that way to learn anything ever, and honestly, not many people like that kind of person.

What I'm talking about is that anyone who tries to make something good and unconventional out of their lives will have to be, at the very least, a little bit stubborn. There will be infinite distractions along your path, there will be many people trying to convince you to do something else, or do something differently at every step of the way. A somewhat stubborn character is a must-have for anyone, as it will allow you to avoid being distracted and convinced by the constant stream of doubt, fear and negativity that will, undoubtedly, come towards you at some point.

It's important to differentiate positive stubbornness—which allows you to stay focused and is a tremendous help when dealing with the negative people and things that you encounter along the way—from negative stubbornness, which is more akin to plain arrogance, making it impossible for you to recognize your mistakes and unwilling to look at yourself, and your actions, objectively. And it's not just about shutting down everyone who tries to give you advice or ignoring whatever doesn't fit your way of thinking. It is about having enough self-awareness to detect if those critics have your best interests in mind—in which case you can try to learn something from what they're telling you—or if their opinions are merely useless distractions that you should definitely should, since they will only make you stumble.

Anyone who tries to become better will come across people that want to get them to stop their forward motion. Maybe it's that friend that sits on his ass all day and doesn't want your success to make him feel inadequate, maybe it's a member of your family truly worried about you, or maybe it's someone who knows nothing about you but has such an ego as to feel that he knows what's best for you. If we listened to all of that noise, we'd be left running in circles and getting nowhere. It's important, therefore, to recognize the source and the nature of that noise, to see if there is something helpful to be found in it. If that's the case then you should listen to the advice, and learn. Otherwise ignore it and move on. An arrogant person wouldn't even analyze if the advice could be helpful.

This subtle, confident stubbornness is required in keeping from constantly doubting yourself. You do need to think that you know what's best for you, and that you are in the right path. If that's not the case, chances are that you will always be changing your approach, always thinking you are doing things wrong, always doubtful and insecure when it comes to making important choices, and that's not good at all.

Be humble enough to be on the lookout for improvement opportunities, but confident and stubborn enough to also know when to trust your gut, and to ignore outside voices and distractions that are not positive or that don't really have your best interests in mind. Learn to recognize when it's wise to listen to advice, and when it's better to trust your own knowledge, to know when you actually know something better than someone else and when you don't. It's not about ignoring everyone, and also not about listening to everyone, but rather about developing the ability to discern between when it's worth taking in some advice, and when it's better to simply nod, and ignore the other person's comments.

Synthesis

We are too used to drifting. It's the most common course of action and because of that we consider it to be acceptable. Because most people don't know where they want to go, or don't care enough to act on that purpose, it's seen as normal to ignore the truly pressing questions of life for as long as possible. This is not good. These questions will appear at some point, and the sooner we ask them, the better, for we will have more time to focus our lives and actions on our ideal future.

Another thing that happens quite often is that we know where we want to go and have a general idea about how to do it, but simply cannot break free from all the distractions and bad influences of everyday life. It's important then, both to ask ourselves questions about how we would want our life to be, and set goals and milestones that let us know that we are moving closer to those goals. It's also important to prioritize and privilege those actions that help build our mental image of our future, instead of those that simply satisfy an idle pleasure. Keep your head down and stay focused, know that you know what's better for you and do not let people distract you from your path.

Patience

"For anything worth having one must pay the price; and the price is always work, patience, love, self-sacrifice - no paper currency, no promises to pay, but the gold of real service."
-John Burroughs

Instant gratification

Entitlement is poison. And it has become such a staple of our culture and of my generation that it has become accepted as a valid outlook towards life. We expect things to be given to us. We hide behind the moral high ground of proclaiming the intrinsic value of everything born alive and greedily demand more money, more happiness and more material success from "the world". Who told us that we deserve anything only for existing? That's absolutely pitiful, and it has caused us to forget that nobody owes us anything, and least of all the world itself. Nowadays everyone demands more and more, claiming their right to an ever-growing set of "rights", while doing absolutely nothing to improve their lives, and crying about the world being unfair. And the world is unfair, in many ways, but that is a basic reality that we are just going to have to accept. You want to know how to minimize that? We start telling people that their lives are their responsibility, and we stop the growing culture that establishes entitlement as acceptable. We get people to stop thinking they "deserve" something, and we replace entitlement with hard work, to get people to understand that things are earned through effort and suffering, and not given freely to anyone that simply desires them and feels they have a claim to them. Instant gratification is a natural, direct consequence of entitlement. Thinking that we deserve everything we want will undoubtedly breed the childish desire to receive everything immediately, and cause us to become impatient. Pair this with the fact that technology has taken tremendous steps towards guaranteeing that we almost never have to wait much for anything, and you're left with a generation that isn't used to having to work and wait for absolutely anything, and expect things to manifest themselves magically—and quickly.

People will go to the gym for a few weeks, expecting to look like a bodybuilder after, and quit when they realize that getting a well-built body will take a massive amount of effort and patience. People will try to build a business and quit when they realize that they're not going to be millionaires in a year. People will want something, and never dedicate more than a minimal amount of time and effort to trying to get it. No matter how much the world progresses, there are some things that will never be easily attainable, and they are usually the truly important things in life. Remember this, or you too will be caught in the growing culture of impatience, and of lack of perseverance.

Impatience doesn't only lead to us quitting when

things take more time than we anticipated, which is sufficiently bad by itself, but it also makes daily life a stressing and grueling matter in which every time we have to wait for something we whine and cry about it like bratty children. We've forgotten the importance of waiting, of being patient, of knowing that valuable things require much time, effort, perseverance and patience to be accomplished. Don't let instant gratification trick you into thinking otherwise, for that will only lead to you becoming a quitter, and quitters never accomplish anything of value.

Aggressive patience

Aggressiveness is a virtue. Let me explain that before it is misinterpreted: Aggressiveness is different from violence, and it definitely doesn't mean starting quarrels with anyone who gives you a funny look. Aggressiveness, in the sense that I am using it here, is the opposite of passiveness, of laziness. It's action, it's determined forward motion. It's about getting things done over and over again, not complaining, and not quitting. It's making things happen, not waiting for them to happen magically. Aggressiveness means tackling the problems of life with a can-do mentality, it means not stopping when trouble arises, it means being able to work and work even if results don't manifest themselves immediately. It means being able to keep your head down and work your ass off, it means not wasting your life watching TV and being lazy, but rather getting up every single day with enough courage and drive to pursue your goals and dreams.

It's also important to define patience. Patience is not the act of lying down and waiting for things to come to you. It's not wishing for things and hoping they will eventually come true. Patience, true patience is the ability to recognize that your dreams won't come quickly, that a worthy life and any valuable project take time to be built. Patience means knowing not to quit when things don't happen exactly when you wished they would. Because things of value don't come without effort, it is necessary to undertake—with aggressive patience—the actions required to make them become a reality. That means working towards them every day, never stopping and never quitting. Do not get discouraged if you aren't a millionaire by the end of the year, do not get sad and quit if you haven't lost all the weight you wanted to lose this month, do not stop working if your business hasn't taken off. Remember that perseverance is what truly differentiates those who make it from those who don't. Heck, it may take you twenty years or it may take you three months. It will be worth it in the end, but whatever it is you are pursuing won't come unless you aggressively work to get it, every day.

Make of aggressive patience a way of life, and you will undoubtedly get—sooner or later—to where you want to get. Just keep working, don't desist, and patiently wait for your goals to become a reality.

Pay your dues

The greatest fulfillment doesn't come from getting things easily, but by achieving those goals that have pushed us to our limit, by finally accomplishing, after suffering the most grueling despair and disappointment, those dreams that have forced us to work endlessly. We learn much when we have to work to get something that is important to us. We learn to be strong, we learn to persevere, we learn the true value of hardships and we learn to appreciate and respect everything that took time to be built.

Those who have never had to sacrifice anything to accomplish something will never understand the pure joy and sense of fulfillment that comes when hard work finally pays off. The thing is, nowadays we aren't forced to pay our dues, for most people don't need to work hard to live relatively comfortable lives, and it has been thus forgotten that the purpose of life is not to live a "comfortable" life, but to find meaning in the pursuit of hard, challenging goals and in the sacrifice that comes naturally from this pursuit.

Because of the generalized comfort of modern life, coupled with instant gratification, many people are completely lost, finding no fulfillment and no meaning in their daily tasks, hating every second of every day and drifting aimlessly in the sea of petty comforts and mediocrity that has become a "normal" life. To escape from this trap, it is wise to understand that that's not the only possible way to live, that it is a real possibility to create whatever kind of life you want, but only if you are willing to sacrifice some things for it, to work hard and stay patient, to keep learning and to fend off discouragement when you think that things aren't working out. It will come, whatever you want, if you pay your dues.

Find meaning in this search and nothing will be powerful enough to stray you from that path, as you will look at everything as a simple challenge to be overcome, not as an indication that you should be doing something else. You will experience the hardships along the way almost joyfully, as they will become landmarks that tell you that what you are pursuing is worthwhile, because if the way is hard, the benefits that you reap at the end, and the things that you learn along the way will be all the more fulfilling. Become comfortable with this reality and you'll start to see the way towards your goals much more clearly, you'll find direction and purpose in the great paradox that overcoming adversity is the greatest pleasure any man can experience.

Synthesis

Lack of patience is a generalized evil that has become characteristic of both our era and our generation. Because of the rate at which technology advances and the ease of being connected and getting things done quickly, we have become accustomed to things happening and appearing almost instantly. The problem is that this then leads to us quitting or getting severely discouraged when things take longer than expected.

It's critical then, to recognize this and take in the fact that many things—mostly things that are actually worth something—require time and effort to materialize. Knowing this, deeply accepting this truth will help us persevere when circumstances are hard. With patience, and aggressive, consistent action, the things that you're pursuing will eventually happen, if only you internalize the value of patience and combine it with focused, purposeful actions towards your goals.

Humility

"Do you wish to rise? Begin by descending. You plan a tower that will pierce the clouds? Lay first the foundation of humility."
- Saint Augustine

It begins with humility

Humility is the virtue that makes it possible for all the other virtues to be learnt. Every single learning process starts with the recognition of a fault, which is something that requires humility. The other requirement is to recognize that the quality we are lacking or ability that we want to learn is important, which is also not very common, as people that lack humility will most likely brush off anything that they do not possess as something unimportant, superficial, or useless. Of course, that is not all that determines whether or not a person is humble, for it reaches much deeper than that. True, sincere humility is admitting your flaws and working to improve them, it's recognizing that your life is not how you want it to be and striving to make it better. It is being well aware of your own limitations and using that awareness as a stepping stone towards building a way of life concentrated on the constant pursuit of learning and on peacefully looking at things objectively. It means not taking things personally, not letting yourself be controlled by your ego and your arrogance, but rather being always able to analyze situations, and your own behavior, and having the balls to accept it when you did something wrong or could've acted somewhat better.

As you can see, once humility becomes your basic behavior, all other virtues will start becoming part of your character, for you'll be able to realize that you could improve here or there, that you are lacking strength and should therefore become stronger, that you are lacking patience and should work on that, that you lack discipline and that it's important to learn how to be more disciplined. These are things that a non-humble person won't even consider, as they will most likely be convinced of the perfection in their ways and everything else will be set aside as useless and unworthy.

It is not enough, however, simply to say "nobody is perfect", and realize that you have some negative things about you. Absolutely everyone does that. But as we've discussed before, merely thinking about stuff is of no use, which is why you have to start taking action and putting into practice that awareness, in the sense of actively looking for errors and seeking a way to solve them. That's how we will start to improve, and that's how humility can be the first step towards creating the person that you ought to be.

Humility is not modesty

When humility is discussed it usually ends up being described as modesty, or frugality, or something acutely similar to those attributes. It's considered humble to live a modest life, not paying too much attention to material success and being mostly at peace with the circumstances that you're currently living. That's absolutely fine, if that is the kind of life that you want. But many people don't want that, because, like it or not, material and financial success is absolutely important, especially nowadays. Having enough money will allow you to give your family a better life, to live without the constant worry of not having enough to pay your bills. As with anything important, those that don't have it will usually try to minimize its importance in order to avoid feeling bad about not having it.

As I've said, if you want to live a modest life, then props to you, but a not so deep observation of the modern world will yield the result of realizing that most people's problems revolve mostly around money. Money is the thing that most worries almost any person in almost any society, because deep down we know that it's important to our peace, and our freedom. Don't let yourself be convinced by those that claim that the pursuit of financial success is a "superficial" or "material" thing. And definitely don't buy into the common myth that decrees that rich (whatever "rich" actually means) people are by definition "arrogant" or selfish. The value and character of a person has nothing to do with their financial capabilities. A modest person is not necessarily humble, and a person that lives a luxurious lifestyle can also be extremely generous.

The pursuit of money is not an immoral thing. If your aim is to be able to give back, think about how much more you could donate to charity if you were rich. If your goal is to have a happy family, think about how much more you will be able to provide for your children if your financial situation were better. Whatever your driver is, money will enhance it. If we look at things that way, all of a sudden money stops being a thing of evil and becomes something that will make your noble purposes a reality, and which will allow you to help a lot more people than if you hadn't any. The point that I'm trying to make is the following: humility has nothing to do with how much money you make. Humility is a virtue of you character, not the expression of your financial means. Modesty is neither a good nor a bad thing; it's simply a way of living that suits some people. They are different concepts. In any case, I personally believe the pursuit of financial success moral, as it will help me provide a happier, more peaceful life for my children and my family.

Don't feel guilty if the life that you imagine for yourself includes expensive cars and a big house. That's respectable, as long as you get there ethically. But desiring those things is not evil. If that's something that you want to pursue, then go for it. Don't let other people tell you that it's greedy to want wealth. More often than not, those are the same people that demand free things from the government and are always complaining about not having enough money. It's normal to want to live a financially comfortable life, as it is undeniable that it brings a lot of benefits for you and for others that you care about.

Differentiating between the concepts of modesty

and humility is key, because otherwise you'd be left feeling guilty for wanting to earn more money, and would end up thinking that the moral thing to do is to not pursue more wealth, forgetting that humility and modesty are completely different values, independent of one another.

Control your ego

Lots of people are talking and writing about the ego, and the general consensus seems to be that the ego is a horrible thing and we should completely eradicate it from our personality. And while it's wise to know that most of our relationships suffer from ego problems, blatantly defining the ego as negative is tricky because many people can misunderstand the well-intended advice to get rid of their egos as meaning they should avoid confrontation completely, and basically just accept being pushovers that never react or defend their honor or integrity. That is a huge mistake, and a costly one, because if that is how you start acting, over time you'll be completely incapable of standing up for yourself, avoiding every type of conflict, even when justified. You don't want that to happen, as letting people push you over is a definite road towards living an unhappy, resentful life. The ego is not always a negative thing, nor is pride, nor is having a sense of honor. However, all those things need to be managed so that they become positive features of your character, and not a counterproductive and angry set of behaviors.

This, as everything else, requires humility. It is first necessary to do an exercise in introspection—something that only a humble person can do, because the process of becoming self-aware of our flaws hurts—to find situations in which our egos got the best of us and had us reacting emotionally and irrationally. But it is from this analysis that we can then discern when having a sense of pride is useful and when it isn't. As an example, let's consider two situations. Imagine, first, that you've put a lot of time and effort into a project and someone tells you—not to hurt you, but honestly letting you know their opinion—that it's not that good. In this situation, the emotional reaction would be to get offended and tell the other person that they know nothing, that you know better and get angry at them. Even if your reaction isn't that extreme, it will hurt your relationship with that person, and they'll think twice about giving you their feedback next time. The humble reaction would be to thank them for their input and analyze what you could have done better. That's a situation where controlling your ego and your pride is a good thing. The second situation is one in which people intentionally attack your honor, your family, or other things important to you. In those cases, the right thing to do may be to firmly let them know that this sort of purposeless criticism is unacceptable. It's highly likely that people that do attack you are hiding their true cowardice behind a façade of aggressive behavior, and are trying to measure how far they can push you before you stop them, which means that a firm statement of disapproval will, in many cases, end the problem right there. This is something that is common in bullying cases, in which the victim is not always attacked due to incapacity to defend themselves, but also due to the fact that they won't fight back. In that sense, trying to play the spiritual superstar and preach peace in a completely ego-less way will be counterproductive, as some people are simply idiots, and will keep pushing you until you stop them.

Control your ego enough to not be the guy that gets offended and hurt by every little disparaging comment, the guy that holds grudges forever and lives a bitter, sad life in his own head. This will bring you more peace than you can imagine, as you'll be free from the emotional drama and petty pains of always having your feelings hurt and always trying to defend your weak self-esteem. But don't be the guy that lets everyone walk all over him, that never defends himself or his people for fear of conflict. Find balance and the correct amount of ego in your life, learn to keep it in check and you'll be respected for your ability to control yourself and your emotions, and for the strength and pride with which you defend your values and your loved ones.

It's honorable to start from the bottom

One of the most damaging expressions of arrogance is the one in which people are absolutely unwilling to take up work that they perceive to be "below them". Not only is this a mindset that clearly demonstrates immense entitlement, but it's also wrong to forget that it's possible to find meaning and purpose in even the simplest of works.

The wisest people know that the top can only be reached by starting at the very bottom, and that those who get everything suddenly are much more likely to waste it away. Why do you think most lottery winners go back to being broke after a while? They didn't pay their dues. They didn't earn their way to the top, financially speaking. This principle applies to much more than personal finances, as in every endeavor that we chose to engage in we will be forced to begin at the very bottom, and start working and learning our way to the top. It's a universal law that what comes quickly and easily leaves like that as well. Building something from nothing, over time and through effort is the only way to construct something that will last.

Don't misunderstand what I'm saying. If the opportunity presents itself to start higher it may be a good idea to take it, but you always have to be willing and ready to start at the bottom again, as nothing is guaranteed. This mindset will be your safety net, as even in the worst of circumstances you'll know yourself capable of rising and advancing—and will thus not be held back by the fear of losing what you've earned.

There is honor in starting at the bottom, it's the sign of a humble person, of one capable of accepting they lack experience and need to start learning as everyone else. Don't fall into the trap of thinking that because of your upbringing, education or financial position you're entitled to avoid paying your dues and think that you're owed a better position or something better than what you have.

Be the man that is willing to grow slowly, be the one that understands the impossibility of easy success, thus ignoring this futile pursuit for quick enrichment in favor of a life of hard work and finding meaning in learning and in the process of slowly and patiently building something worthy.

Do everything with purpose

We are often presented with some task or obligation that seems useless, and we tend to treat it as such, ignoring it for as long as possible, then performing it half-heartedly and mediocrely, and feeling satisfied with the average outcome. I myself am also guilty of this behavior. But I've come to understand that there is no such thing as a petty task or useless obligation, for they are always important in the sense that they bring some benefit when done purposefully and done right—for instance the benefit of actually learning to do things right, however small they may be, and learning to treat every obligation with respect.

The problem with getting used to doing things in a mediocre fashion is that, as creatures of habit, we get used to this kind of behavior, which in turn means that not even those tasks that deserve our full attention will get completed as well as they could be.

It's a terrible thing to believe the excuse that "this task is not important, and therefore not doing it properly is justified", because your brain will find ways to apply that same excuse to bigger and bigger tasks, until nothing you do gets done well and you become accustomed to mediocrity.

Do everything with purpose, undertake every single thing in your life as if it were a matter of life and death, and do not fall into the trap of being mediocre under the excuse of the task being unimportant. Do this and you'll be more than ready when it's time to perform on the big stage, when the big project is to be completed, for you'll be used to the pressure of trying to do things to the best of your ability, which will mean that no task will be big enough and important enough to overwhelm you.

How you do the small things is also how you do the big, crucial things, and that is a principle that you should always keep in mind. Remember it, use it to your advantage, and start performing at your very best in all areas of your life, for no task is ever unimportant.

Synthesis

Humility is the virtue that allows for any and every improvement to take place. The capacity of critically analyzing our actions and thoughts is what will in turn trigger, through corrective action, change.

Humility is what allows us to start from the bottom with a proud look on our faces. Humility is what gives us the capacity to recognize when we've done wrong, and to become better human beings from this recognition. Humility is what will keep our mind open to new teachings and different ways of thinking. Being humble means being able to control our ego when it matters, to save time, energy, and sometimes even money pursuing useless fights for the sake of pride.

Practice humility and there will be no limit to how much your character can grow, to how great you can truly be.

Loyalty

"Never esteem anything as of advantage to you that will make you break your word or lose your self-respect."

- Marcus Aurelius

You are your best friend

We are all alone in this world. Sure, most of us have close friends, family, or at least some acquaintances that accompany us most of the time, but none of them will be constantly holding our hand for the rest of our life. The only person that will always be a constant part of your life is you. This is a simple fact, and most of us know it. And yet, we usually don't act according to this fundamental truth of existence. We tend to become our own worst enemy, forgetting that there is no one else cheering for us, that people are not going to support us all the time, and that if we turn against ourselves, we will have no way of progressing.

Even your own subconscious will try to bring you down. How many times do we let ourselves into that vicious circle of self-pity and negativity? How often do we beat ourselves down, overestimating our flaws and failures? The answer is, way too often. But the great thing about being a human being is that we have the capacity for rational thought, which means that we can choose not to let our subconscious determine how we think, act and feel. Do not let yourself be guided by emotions and feelings of doubt and self-pity. You can control your mind and tell it to shut up and stop whining, for you know your worth.

Because of the fact that you cannot—and indeed shouldn't—depend on anyone else for support and motivation, it is absolutely paramount that you become your biggest supporter, and that you use your mind as a tool that can propel you forward.

Otherwise you are shooting yourself in the foot, beating yourself down instead of using your mind to your advantage. It doesn't make any sense to handicap yourself voluntarily by not controlling your very own mind.

There is no one else but you, and this will become evident at some point in everyone's life. No one can escape from this and therefore we must make our peace with that fact and start working towards independence of thought and action, so that when that grueling loneliness comes creeping your way, you'll be trained not to give in to despair and feelings of doubt and fear, and be able to control your mind and push yourself forward, encouraging and motivating yourself to get out of that dark hole.

Loyalty is not freely given

We live in a globalized era. The world is now more connected than ever, and we are constantly being told that we are to behave as citizens of the world and that everyone is our friend and deserving of our respect and loyalty. It's not realistic to think that someone can be equally loyal to everyone, as it's a natural thing for any living being to form closer ties with some, and to be loyal to a certain group of people first. That's not immoral.

That mentality makes it difficult to establish priorities, because embracing this feel good dogma in which everyone is equally important in our eyes leads us to feel immoral when having to choose someone's well-being over the well-being of another person or another group. Once we accept the fact that no one truly cares for everyone equally, nor is it a moral obligation to do so, we can become more honest with ourselves and with our priorities, as we'll be free to recognize why, and for whom we do the things that we do, who we want to help the most and how we are going to do that. Accepting that it's normal to put your family and your friends first will make you stop wasting time and energy trying to please people that you don't really like and that don't care about you, and direct your efforts towards improving the lives of those that have made your life better, that care about your wellbeing, and that deserve your loyalty.

Simple as that may seem, most people don't take that into account when deciding how to spend their time and energy. How many young boys and girls have been misled into living completely fake lifestyles, almost exclusively focused on trying to "fit in", and trying to behave like a "cool" person, and then end up mistreating and disparaging their families and those who care about them? It's almost like we're caught in a never-ending adolescence, forgetting the values of family and of loyalty towards the people that have made us what we are.

Fake lives, fake friends, and fake people is what we are creating and becoming as a society. It's amazing how much people talk behind other people's backs, as if being a hypocrite were the right thing to do. I'm not saying you should just go ahead and openly hate and confront everyone that you dislike, but that you should be aware of which people are actually deserving of your time and start cultivating those relationships first, before trying to be everybody's best friend.

Your time and your energy are precious, so don't go around wasting it with people that care nothing about you. Recognize who is actually deserving of your loyalty and start being there for them, start spending more time with them, thank them for what they've done for you, don't fall into the trap of forgetting those that built you up in favor of those that weren't there when you needed them. Don't try to care about everyone equally, for not only is that impossible, but it also doesn't benefit anyone, as you'll end up neglecting those that deserve your effort.

Be loyal to yourself

Your well-being comes first, and that is not egoism. Why is it that altruism gets put up in a pedestal? Truly, what logic is there behind thinking that you should put your dreams and ambitions last? When did it become immoral to prioritize our happiness and our peace? Now, now, don't misunderstand me and think I'm telling you to absolutely neglect everyone else to get what you want. I'm simply stating that there will often come a time when you are going to have to make some decisions for the sake of doing what brings you more peace and what you think is more beneficial for you, and that you shouldn't feel bad for putting yourself first in those situations. After all, the only person that is guaranteed to be with you always, is yourself.

We've talked about acting according to your goals, and this is not too different from that, in the sense that the way forward is to remain loyal to what you think is right, to be true to your set of values and to the life that you want to build. While it may seem obvious, behaving like this is harder than you think, as not straying from your path will require large amounts of self-awareness to recognize what is and what isn't consistent with your beliefs. If it were easier, everyone would be living the life that they wanted, and everyone would be completely honest and happy, which isn't the case.

Inconsistency between what we believe and the way we actually act is, in my opinion, one of the greatest sources of unhappiness and the thing that leads most people to feel lost and confused. I mean, it is as if your whole subconscious was telling you to behave a certain way, the right way, and you decided to act completely opposite to that. That's sad, if you ask me. It's sad because most of the time we know what we should do, what the right thing to do is, and yet most times we simply can't get it together and act accordingly. No wonder there are so many people that end up having crises and experiencing so much despair. It may be that their mind is telling them to change their path and start doing things differently, to start doing things correctly, and they can't change their set behaviors and can't start acting in a way that will be consistent with their values and their dreams.

Do everything you can to be consistent with your thoughts, to "practice what you preach", if you will. There is no shame in slipping, so long as you recognize your mistake and get back on track with your life. Be loyal to your values and your dreams; don't betray them in favor of idle pleasures or things and people that aren't worth it. Respect the values of other people and help them be loyal to their code. If there is something that is inconsistent with your moral compass, don't engage in it, and if you do, learn from that mistake. Consistency is what will build your mental image of a happy and satisfying life, and temptations will forever be there to try and stop you. Beat them.

Be valuable

I don't think that every human has the same value for the sole reason of having been born. Sure, that doesn't mean that we shouldn't have any fundamental rights when living in a society, but to preach the intrinsic value of a person as a direct consequence of their mere existence on earth is a gateway to ignoring the recognition that people actually earn by doing great deeds. Once we start claiming that everyone is beautiful just the way they are, that we convince ourselves that the value of a human being is an automatic consequence of his mere existence, it becomes really easy to justify bad habits and damaging lifestyles and to utterly disregard the pursuit of any type of self-improvement. Acceptance movements, the elimination of competition and the constant effort to eliminate all objective criteria has consequences that transcend their own purpose, as they are gateways for a way of thinking in which it's easy to justify your senseless decisions and your lack of discipline, protecting them under the false concept of absolute subjectivity. The value of a human being is the value that he creates, it's the impact he has on other people's lives, it's the joy that he brings. And this is obviously not the same for everyone. The value of a person is a direct consequence of his decisions, and there is nothing wrong in thinking that. Political correctness has buried us into a hole in which "everyone and everything is great exactly the way they are". That is absolutely wrong. You are the value you create, the people you inspire, the deeds that you accomplish, the challenges that you overcome, the progress that you make, the people that you help and the person that you become.

On that note, remember that your present decisions, not your past, are what determine your future. We've discussed this in the responsibility chapter, but it leads into loyalty as well, in a more abstract sense, meaning that being loyal to yourself also means being able to overcome your previous experiences in the pursuit of a better future. Being loyal to yourself means respecting yourself enough to do everything you can to not be a slave of the past, and to have the will to endure and overcome the challenges that are placed in front of you.

You determine your own value. You decide how far you go; you decide what you are on the most essential level. It is up to you either to be a valuable person or someone that lets his potential go to waste and never pushes back, never tries and never accomplishes. Choose wisely.

Synthesis

Loyalty, in the sense that I'm discussing here, is not merely the separation and prioritization of certain people over others, but also a practice of consistency between thought and action, between an established set of priorities and decision making, and between where we want to go and who we want to be and the steps that we can take to get there.

Loyalty also means recognizing that at the most essential level we are all alone—and must therefore become our very own best friends—and that we should aim to control our mind so that it doesn't act against us—loyalty means we use our capacity for rational and conscious thought to advance our interests.

This means recognizing our flaws and working to improve them, being aware that the value of a person is by and large not intrinsic but is rather a combination of his or her set of values, accomplishments, and actions. Loyalty to yourself means doing everything you can to improve and realize your potential, to inspire people through your unwavering strength, discipline and courage, to help others through kindness and truth.

Courage

"Courage is a kind of salvation."

-Plato

Step up

One thing that completely separates people that are on the path to greatness of character and spirit from those that are not is having the ability and courage not to shy away from challenges and tasks because of their perceived difficulty. Nowadays we can get away with avoiding things that seem hard to learn or overcome, because contemporary life often allows us to lead relatively comfortable lives without exerting much effort. Thus, when we have the choice either to face a challenging situation that will lead to growth, or simply avoid the hassle of engaging in it, we tend to choose the second option, because it's easy to rationalize the first option as being "unnecessary" by doing a simple cost/benefit analysis. However logical that decision may appear at first, a deeper look will yield a different result: the benefits of stepping up to do something that no one else will are not only the direct results of accomplishing that action or task, but also, and more importantly, the little bit of mental fortitude and audacity that you learn as a result of being able to face your fears.

There is intrinsic value in simply being able to step up to challenging situations. Volunteering to perform the tasks that make everyone uncomfortable—and of course this doesn't mean putting ourselves blindly at risk—is a fantastically and easily available way of growing as a person. It's the most basic form of "facing your fears", and it will be the beginning of your conquest over those actually important and damaging fears.

Step up when everyone else is shying away from those challenges. You'll later figure out the "how", but learn to have the guts to raise your hand boldly when everyone else is trying their hardest to avoid taking the lead.

Be bold

There is no easier way to waste your life than cowardly waiting for things to happen. There is no surest path to failure and a purposeless life than being satisfied with the unfulfilling circumstances of your life.

As humans, we tend to find more comfort in routine and in knowing what's ahead of us and feel uncomfortable in the face of uncertainty. It's only natural to try and do everything we can to devoid our life of extreme change and create a world in which the future can become a little bit more certain. It's dangerous to let those feelings control your mind and your actions, mainly for two reasons: first, the future is, by definition, plagued by uncertainties. Sure, you can prepare for it, you can try to predict it, but it's impossible to know of any future event with absolute certainty. Second, trying to circumvent the uncertainty of the future will more than likely trap you into thinking that any routine, no matter how bad, is better than change, merely for having the element of certainty built into it. The only time where change isn't useful, or even necessary, is when the circumstances that surround you are adjusted to perfection. That will never be the case, for the world is dynamic, and no set of circumstances can last forever. Also, it isn't realistic to think that you can have every little thing be exactly as you want it to be.

Instead of waiting for the future to kick you suddenly in the teeth, it is much wiser to be bold enough and visionary enough to forge it, to act in such a way that you are actively creating your life and building your future every day. Even if disaster happens and the world changes drastically, you'd have learnt the boldness required to confront your circumstances through action, instead of letting every little change push you over. If life is to punch you in the face, be bold enough to punch back. Make things happen, make change happen! Be prepared to adjust and adapt to whatever life throws at you, but don't ponder for too long and act boldly, because otherwise change will happen faster than your ability to adapt.

Boldness requires courage, action requires courage, and adaptation requires courage. Being willing to change your comfortable routine requires courage and seeking greatness requires courage, but all of those things are absolutely worth it. Winning requires courage.

On "safe spaces"

I honestly don't understand how so many people are actually pushing for the creation of "safe spaces", where no one will be "judged" or criticized or challenged in any way. Are we so utterly disconnected from reality that we are demanding a plastic representation of a utopian fantasy where we can purposefully be weak and childlike and where no one can tell us that we are hurting ourselves? Where we can hide from the reality that betterment is a consequence of mistakes, and of recognizing our flaws? Have we really become so weak that we need somebody else's aid to protect us from <u>words</u>?

I know what some people may be thinking: bullying is real and some kids suffer serious damage from being picked on and words can really harm them. That's true. But I'm not talking about kids. And I'm not talking about those situations when someone actually sets out to hurt another person, even though it's smart to arm ourselves against that as well. I'm talking about grown adults that are so whiny that they think they are entitled to demand protection when someone disagrees with their life choices, opinions and decisions. If you think that's an exaggeration, you're wrong. That's actually happening. People are demanding actual physical spaces where they can be "safe", not from actual threats and danger, but from words, ideas and people that make them feel uncomfortable.

Come on, man. That scenario seriously looks like something out of a dystopian novel. Common sense would tell us to react to things that make us uncomfortable by getting stronger, not by cowardly waiting for the world to become nicer. Put your big boy pants on and when something or someone is making you feel bad, fight back. Stand up taller. Learn how to take it in and grow from it. Courage can be built when we are facing problems and when we are feeling somehow scared. Be courageous and learn how to face the hard situations of life, learn how to deal with people that want to hurt you, because such things will always be there, and fantasizing about a perfectly peaceful and inoffensive world will not make them go away. What will make them go away is your capacity to face them head on and your ability to take all of those challenges in and learning how to deal with them. Safe spaces don't exist, and never will.

Have the courage to create

Courage can only exist in the face of some kind of risk. Because of the limited physical threats that are to be found in today's modern world, the physical realm is usually not the place where courage is most easily seen. Of course some physical threats still exist and will continue to exist, and we should be ready for them as well, but there is also a different type of courage, one that happens when we risk our social standing or our emotional state in the pursuit of something we believe to be right.

Every person who has ever built something great, every creator who has made some beautiful work will be heavily criticized and even hated by some. That criticism is, more often than not, simply a defense mechanism used by people who feel inadequate when they see another person achieve what they themselves couldn't, or simply won't achieve. We all do this to various degrees. How often have you tried to brush off someone else's achievement by deeming it easy or unimportant, and knowing deep down that that's not the case? How many times have we secretly been envious of someone that is receiving praise for his work, telling ourselves and those around us that we could've done that as well?

This thought process is a negative feedback loop that keeps us stuck in inaction, induced by fear of criticism, and makes us criticize anyone that isn't letting themselves be crippled by fear, and are actually creating valuable things. It's imperative to break free from this cycle, one, by respecting the courage required to try to create something, and two, by attempting it ourselves.

Creating isn't the exclusive purview of artists, musicians, painters or sculptors. In any profession you may be in, you're a creator of something. And even if that's not the case, you're the creator of you. You are the one that creates your personality, your name, your life. That can also be a work of art. Your mere existence can inspire people to be better; your simple presence can have a positive impact on those around you. You don't have to be an outlier, for in each human being exists the power to create something of extreme beauty.

Creation demands courage. Not all works are beautiful, but if we keep trying, they will eventually be. Critics will be there no matter the quality of what you create, so don't beat yourself up too much if the first version of your creation isn't perfect, for it will be better next time you try.

Be courageous enough to pursue the creation of beautiful works, of a beautiful personality, of a beautiful life. Try to create something that will inspire those that look at it. Every single one of us has the power to inspire at least one other person, and that's the worst-case scenario. Chances are that your efforts will be recognized by many, and that number will keep growing with time if you don't let mean words and hatred distract you from the fact that you are on the path of greatness. Walking that path and failing is a hundred times better than walking the comfortable one where no one cares about you and succeeding at it.

Pursue what you believe to be right, and create something that resembles those values, that can transmit your vision to other people, that can inspire them to pursue their own dream and be creators themselves.

Walk into the fire

You will never be prepared enough for anything. None of us will. And yet, perceived lack of preparation is what usually leads us to rejecting opportunity when it comes our way. I'll give you an example: yesterday I was approached to give a twenty-minute talk to an audience of over a hundred people. The details are not important; the only important things to know are as follows: I'd never before spoken in front of so many people (or done any sort of public speaking for that matter), I had to prepare a twenty minute talk (which feels like an eternity) in less than fourteen hours, having arrived from a month-long trip that same day. It was very evident I wasn't prepared at all. And yet, I said yes immediately, and banged out a fifteen-minute (didn't manage to get twenty minutes) talk as best as I could with the circumstances as they were. And it went well. It didn't go perfectly, but it went well. It was a very cool experience, and I'm grateful I said yes. This experience, which happened yesterday, motivated me to write this section. In front of me I had every excuse in the book not to do this talk, and yet I knew that this was an opportunity that I had to seize. So I did, without knowing how I was going to do it.

We tend to opt out of opportunities that we fear are too big for us, too difficult, or simply too scary, and justify it by saying we are not fully prepared. But that ends up snowballing into a life in which we always feel that we must be better prepared for any situation, and we end up getting paralyzed. There is value in being prepared. I'm not asking you to throw every sort of preparation out of the window and proceed to improvise everything. That's not good. But it's just as bad to avoid engaging in anything for fear of being "not ready".

I'm saying: when opportunity presents itself, seize it. Accept the challenge and do your very best to learn along the way. Prepare if you can, but doing it is always better than not doing it. Sometimes you won't have time to get ready, to practice as much as you'd like and to research and analyze every little detail. On those occasions, just say yes, and worry afterwards about how you're going to perform. Commit first, seize the opportunity and learn as you go. That's how you really learn: by throwing yourself out there and forcing yourself to figure things out. As I've said, prepare as you can, but never let lack of preparation be your reason for rejecting a potential opportunity.

Synthesis

Lethargy is a much larger dream killer than lack of opportunity or lack of preparation. We are becoming lethargic in the way we do things, in the way we work, act, and even think. It's much easier to lazily and cowardly satisfy ourselves with the bare minimum and never have the courage to walk into the fire to try and get something worthy out of life.

Any and every worthy achievement and creation will require courage and willingness to experience disappointment, failure, or even pain. It will demand boldness and persistence from you, and you will be tested at every step of the process. But trying and failing is a thousand times better than not even pursuing that goal for fear of not succeeding or being ridiculed.

Pursue your dreams boldly and fearlessly and have the courage to seize every opportunity that crosses your path, and remember that the discomfort that you'll experience on this pursuit won't ever go away, so it's better to get used to it.

Kindness

"No act of kindness, no matter how small, is ever wasted."

-Aesop

Kindness

This chapter will probably contrast strongly with the previous caffeine-and-metal induced chapters, but that will hopefully make it even more impactful. If you've kept reading up to this point, thank you. I guess you found some value in my words, because otherwise you would've thrown the book in the thrash. The other option, less likely but also possible, is that you hate the things I've said and are trying to gather as much information as possible so you can criticize me. I appreciate both of those outlooks.

I placed this chapter at the end of the book on purpose: I believe that any person that has read through the somewhat controversial previous chapters deserves to read what I'm about to write. All of those that have given up and simply stopped reading will not know that this chapter will (hopefully) render most criticism misplaced. If not, no problem. I truly look forward to what people have to say.

The virtues in this book are not listed in any sort of order. I just wrote them as I went on. But this one was always going to be at the end. If you are reading this then you most likely took this book as something positive and not as an empty rant. If you are reading this, I believe that my words were not misunderstood and that the positive message of becoming a disciplined, strong and responsible person are what you'll remember from this book. If that's the case, this chapter won't be contradictory at all, but will be perfectly in line with my previous thoughts, and I know that you'll see that clearly. People that know me know that kindness is a virtue that I pursue with the same determination as the other ones; that I truly wish to help people and that I find great joy when I get to help somebody make his or her life better.

This book says the things it says, and is written in this specific manner, for a reason, which is that I don't believe kindness to be the same as making someone feel good. In my eyes, kindness is trying to help people be better and happier in a deeper way, and in some cases that happens when you say things directly and in a more impactful way. At least that's how it works for me. I am grateful for those books that have given me a firm slap across the face and woken me up from my lethargy, allowing me to take the wheel and live a better, more fulfilling life.

None of the virtues I preach are in any way contradictory to the practice of kindness as a way of life; in fact, they are all values that will help you boost the positive impact that you can have on people, by becoming a more influential and more honest person. That's the actual purpose of this book. I decided to write it as I did because I would've liked to have someone tell me those things in that fashion a whole lot earlier, and I believe that the way I did it is the most accurate way to depict and transmit the message of strength that I've been trying to communicate.

Never forget the value of honest acts of kindness. When your default setting is to be kind to people (and this doesn't being naïve or a pushover), your relationships will improve greatly, you'll connect to people on a deeper level, you'll understand them and understand yourself in the process. There's no reason not to help someone when you can. But remember that helping is not necessarily doing what they want or saying what will make them feel good.

Hope

Hope

Many of the thoughts contained in this book may
have looked grim to you. I understand that. That
served the purpose of portraying (accurately) the
circumstances that we, as humans, have faced, are
facing, or will undoubtedly face at some point in our
journey. The darkness and evil that exist in this
world are unmeasurable, and it is better to come to
that conclusion through analysis and self-reflection

than by witnessing it firsthand. While none of us is exempt from encountering a circumstance that certifies the human capacity for evil, beign aware of that possibility and preparing for it can help us avoid it somehow. That was the purpose of the paragraphs in which I tried to depict the reality of a world that one way or another will bring suffering our way.

However, my intent was never to make you lose hope in the possibility of betterment for you, society, or the world as a whole, for I truly believe that inside of us there is as much potential for good as for bad. I believe in the power of a single person trying to help another, in the ripples that a single good action can have. At the end of the day, that has always been the purpose of this book, and I honestly hope that you understood it in that fashion.

I believe that through strength, discipline and kindness we can lift ourselves up from even the deepest hole and inspire other people to do the same. I believe it is right to hope for a better, stronger world. I believe that inspiring and motivating other people to grow and improve—to outperform themselves—is how we can start creating a better, happier future for everyone.

Final thoughts

This has been a tough book to write. Unlike my previous books, this was not a practical guide, but rather a recounting of my own view of the world. Because it contains so much of myself, and because of the way it's written, I've found myself wondering for far more time than before how people would react to the words it contains. Many possible scenarios have crossed my mind, ranging from extreme success to the most devastating of misinterpretations and criticism. The likelihood is that there will be mixed reactions, for anything that is worth something is usually also criticized. I guess that I'll have to find peace in the knowledge that every word in this book was written with the main purpose of helping my readers and bringing some good into the world through writing.

I've revised this work more times over than any of the previous ones, trying to perfect every single detail into creating something that accurately depicts what I'm trying to communicate, trying to imagine how people reading the book would feel and twisting and turning words so that the predominant feelings in any reader's mind would be inspiration, motivation, and the certainty of reading something that comes from a place of honesty and genuine desire to help anyone find their path in this life.

Uncertainty about the reactions of whoever reads what I've written still persist in my mind, but as I've said before: if this book helps even one person, I'll consider it a success, which is why I'm willing to risk the criticism and negative reactions that could be coming my way. If they come, so be it. I'm fully aware and stand by the things I've said but I am also open to listening to any thought that contradicts my way of thinking. Feel free to write me an email at juan-dominguez7@hotmail.com, or to contact me through my Instagram page @juandominguezdelcorral.

All that is left to say is that I hope you found in this book the little push that you needed to start moving forward, to become aggressive in your pursuit of truth, success, and the future that you want. I also hope that you enjoyed it and that it added value to your life. It took time, effort, persistence, and honestly, a lot of courage to publish this and release the contents of my mind into the world in such an open way, and I hope that it was worth it. My biggest dream and my greatest accomplishment would be to have created a work of beauty, something valuable that may forever exist in your memory.

Thank you.

Two cents

- Sleep at least 7 hours every night

- Don't smoke, and control your drinking

- Drink your coffee black

- Read as much as possible

- Lift weights at least 4 times a week

- Metal music is pure energy

- Don't wear gloves in the gym

- Don't be so concerned with your hair

- Plan your days ahead

➤ Meet often with your friends

➤ Family first

➤ Meditate

➤ Complaining helps no one, look for solutions

➤ Take cold showers

➤ Value your family, they are there to help you

➤ Don't seek money, seek freedom

➤ Don't talk about your ideas, make them real instead

➤ Find the largest burden that you can bear, and bear it (Jordan B. Peterson)

- ➢ Stop looking at your phone all the time

- ➢ Help people

- ➢ Details matter

- ➢ What you eat, drink, watch and listen to has an impact on the person you are. Hard things will make you hard, soft things will make you soft.

- ➢ Growth can be a life purpose in itself

- ➢ Seek to learn from every situation

- ➢ Above all, be better

Also by the author

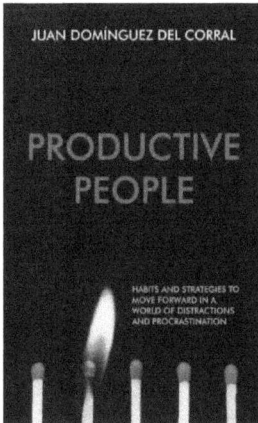

Productive People: *Habits and strategies to move forward in a world of distractions and procrastination.*

- Available on Amazon.com and directly through the author at @juandominguezdelcorral on Instagram

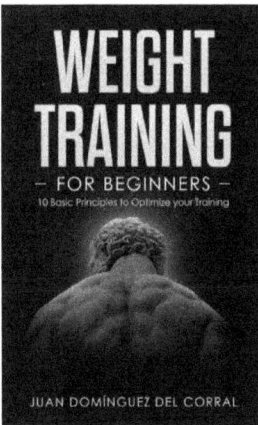

Weight Training for Beginners: *10 Basic Principles to Optimize your Training.*

- Available on Amazon.com and directly through the author at @juandominguezdelcorral on Instagram

"The ultimate measure of a man is not where he stands in moments of comfort and convenience, but where he stands at times of challenge and controversy."

-Martin Luther King, Jr.

www.ingramcontent.com/pod-product-compliance
Lightning Source LLC
LaVergne TN
LVHW041320080426
835513LV00008B/523

9789584876461